Re-singles Rule(s)!

How to Live as a Single in a World of Pairs

Wynora Womack Freeman, Ed. D.
Author, *Re-Singled Is Not a Four-Letter Word: How to Live after Death, Divorce, or a Breakup*

Re-singles Rule(s)!
Copyright 2015 Dr. Wynora Womack Freeman
All rights reserved.

ISBN-13: 978-1500892142
ISBN-10: 1500892149
Also available in eBook

Cover Design: Elizabeth E. Little, Hyliian Graphics,
          www.hyliian.deviantart.com
Interior Design: The Author's Mentor,
          www.LittleRoniPublishers.com
Cover Image Copyright: www.123rf.com/
          somkku9kanokwan

Author Contact: wynoradwf@yahoo.com

PUBLISHED IN THE UNITED STATES OF AMERICA

Also by Wynora Womack Freeman

Re-Singled Is Not a Four-Letter Word: How to Life after Death, Divorce, or a Break-up

Re-singled. All of us will at one point or another become re-singled! When the unthinkable happens—we lose a spouse due to death, divorce, or a break-up, we, the survivors, dwell for a time in relationship purgatory. We must learn to navigate this transitional period. We must deal with a myriad of experiences, anxieties, and societal pressures that being re-singled brings. Let me show you how to escape from purgatory and live a soulfully satisfying life as a re-singled—if only for a season! Buy your copy of Re-singled Is Not a Four-Letter Word today. Available on Amazon.

ontents

Foreword

You are grieving! You are upset, angry, or confused, and rightly so. You have lost a spouse, a partner, or a lover. You miss him terribly, and not only that, you are also suffering from the loss of a relationship. If married, you mourned the loss with the cultural rituals of a funeral or memorial service, a graveside home-going celebration, or a cremation. Surrounded by family, friends, and coworkers, you managed your loss. If divorced, there were no formalized rituals to comfort you. So, you created your own. With the help of others, or your favorite comfort foods, you managed to return to a sense of normalcy, somehow. If you broke off an engagement or ended a long-term relationship, your paths were similar.

During another phase, you noticed that you did not cry as often or as long. You began to see images of your former self. Smiles returned. Your eyes were less red. You began to take pleasure in previous pursuits. You comforted a friend during his loss, or you shared in the joy of another's engagement. You began to notice that you were beginning to feel better. . .

And now? How do you feel about your loss right now? Are you stuck in a quagmire of grief? For every step towards recovery, do you take three backwards? How do you get out? How do you navigate the journey of being a re-singled adult? I know that you didn't plan for this! None of us do. How could we? Nor did you ever imagine that you would be among the 1 million adults who report losing a spouse every year (Social Security Administration). I certainly didn't. But I am a re-singled adult, and so are you—at least for this season.

Never would you in your wildest, most bizarre dreams ever believe that you, yes you, would be at this moment in time a re-singled adult living without a partner. But you are, and yet? Intuitively, you know there's something more. You have caught glimpses of a life that you want for yourself. And deep down inside, you know it's possible. You have seen other widows embrace their losses and move on, emerging more beautiful and more vibrant than ever. You want that. But you are really not sure just what that is or how to get it. Perhaps, it's time for a transformation.

But before we begin, you have to be certain that you are ready, willing, and able to take on the tasks that will demand that you make some changes, think differently, and dare to do. Are you ready to be transformed? Are you sure? Do you want to grow in all dimensions of your life, including spiritually, psychologically, and physically? Are you ready to learn how it's possible to heal from your loss and embrace a future that is uniquely yours? Well, if you are, read on! You are about to embark on a transformative journey. Rules and must-dos, these tools will teach you how to live as a re-singled in a world of pairs, so let the transformation begin!

Introduction

At some point along the continuum of living after loss, we must be willing to experience a renaissance. Depending on whom we ask, a renaissance is a rebirth, revitalization, or a reawakening, a resurgence, or a new start. Historically, the Renaissance refers to the cultural and artistic paradigm shifts that occurred in Europe during the 15th and 16th centuries. During the Renaissance, many believed that man rediscovered, or better still, reinvented himself. In effect, a profound "seismic cultural shift" occurred, and the new discoveries and perspectives continue to impact humankind. As the author of this book, I want you! I want you to own the cosmic shift stirring within your soul and the post-traumatic growth that will occur. You were made in God's image to dominate (Genesis 1:28, KJV*), not to be dominated by your life's circumstances!

I am not attempting to annul the gaping hole in your soul. Once we experience the death of a spouse or a divorce, a part of us shuts down as a result of our relational loss. Vestiges of our selves remain; however, we are somewhat different. Something has changed. Perhaps your life stopped the moment the loss occurred. While the change may be unnoticeable, the effects of losing a spouse or a partner reside deep within; the effects imbue the entire tapestry of our lives.

At this time, you may not be convinced that you will survive your loss. I know; I've had my litany of losses, and I have been where you are. There is one thing I do know, and it is this: if we are going to experience a personal renaissance after relational loss, we need to transform that vision we have unknowingly created for ourselves as newly re-singled adults.

First and foremost, we need to change the way we view our loss, "for as he thinketh in his heart, so is he" (Proverbs 23:7a). If we tend to dwell continuously on our loss, we will be lost.

We will continue to lose and miss out on the gifts of each day. But how do we change our thinking? We can begin by increasing our positive genius potential. According to Shawn Achor in *Before Happiness*, positive geniuses are those who consciously and deliberately create a true reality (one that is believable and doable), rewrite their social scripts, and send their brains positive messages. In effect, to achieve increasingly more happiness and success as a single-again adult, we need to consciously create positive change by rewiring our cognitive circuits!

Research on neuroplasticity—the ability of the brain to change even as an adult—reveals that moderate actions in positive directions can retrain our brains toward positivity. The human brain receives 11 million bits of information per second but can only process 40 bits. Think about this. Of those 40 bits, what percentage of the time do we focus on positive aspects of our re-singled lives and what percentage do we find ourselves dwelling on the negative things that happen to us? According to the positive psychologists, five positive comments are needed to erase the effects of a single negative comment. So for each challenge you may face, show gratitude for the five accomplishments you complete. In fact, Achor posits that success correlates to the extent that we can channel our brains to ferret out and focus on positive opportunities.

As newly re-singled adults, let's focus less on the challenges. Even in the midst of our loss, we need to stop asking "Why?" We may never receive our answer, but we will survive in spite of the pain of our loss. As we heal, the pain lessens. However, just as a broken bone aches in cold weather, so we too may ache when we hear a certain song or a certain memory flashes across our mindscape.

Second, we must be ever mindful of the fact that our realities—our lives right now—are the results of the choices we make, the details of daily living we choose to embrace. Do you get irritated when a driver cuts you off, for example? Pray for her. By doing so, we are focusing on the positive. We will not let that driver steal our joy. In effect, when we concentrate on seeing the big picture and all the positive realities that exist, we become architects of our realities. As re-singles, we are changing our mindsets. When we raise the level of positivity in the present, we are getting back on track. We might not be where we were before the loss, but we are at least in the running. This is crucial! For when a loss first occurs, the only thing we can focus on will be the negative feelings, the pain, and the emptiness. Not convinced? Well, allow me to ask you two questions:

- What is your current reality at this stage as a newly re-singled?
- Is this current reality working for you right now?

If you answered no to the second question, then let's assume you are not living as proactively as you can as a re-singled adult. Is this because you are a little short-sighted right now? Let's transform that vision now.

Transforming the Vision of Yourself as a Re-singled

Habakkuk 2:2-3 states, "And the Lord answered me, and said, Write the vision, and make it plain upon tablets, that he may run that readeth it. For the vision is yet for an appointed time, but at the end it shall speak, and not lie: though it tarry, wait for it; because it will surely come, it will not tarry." Aristotle states that "the soul never thinks without a picture." What do these seemingly disparate quotes have in common? Simply this. They outline the steps for transforming our visions as re-singled adults: first, write the vision and make it plain upon tablets; then think in pictures (images). In other words, we need to craft a personal vision statement, so we will know if we are truly living as God intends for each of us during this season of our singleness.

Understanding Vision

The word "vision" can be applied to any purpose, mission, or goal, even to the particulars in terms of how we choose to live as adults who find ourselves single again. But it's so much more. Like a laser, a vision provides a way of seeing an alternative reality that is true for us. It provides a canvas on which we can paint the picture of what our worlds will look like if our visions came to fruition. Next, a vision is a clear mental image of the results we want to create. It's the compelling idea, fueled by our creative imaginations and inspired by God. Additionally, a vision generates energy, motivates, and assists us in bridging the gap between where we are now and where we want to be as a re-singled adult. Acting as a "success accelerant" (Shawn Achor), our vision will compel us to actively and intently make decisions and choose behaviors based on how to 'get there'. Remember, the vision alone does not generate the staying power to live out our visions of what success looks like for us as re-singles; it merely provides the impetus.

Finally, a vision motivates and empowers us to choose those experiences that will propel us forward as newly re-singled adults. Having a clearly-defined vision will help us persevere in the face of rejections, missteps, and stumbling blocks. A vision stretches us to excel. As Nelson Mandela said, "It always seems impossible until it's done." A vision helps with the doing; it's what happens when the divinely-inspired imagination forges a masterpiece out of the messiness of death, divorce, or a promise shattered.

Vision Statement: Prelude to Transformation

A vision statement will sustain us and bring our vision to fruition. According to Christopher Gergen and Gregg Vanourek, "Our life vision should take our breath away with its audacity. It should roar with passion and set markers for what we plan to do with our days on the planet".[1] In fact, a personal vision statement reflects our core values, our religious beliefs, in other words, the legacy we want to create, share, and bequeath to others. A vision statement usually incorporates a view about how we "see" ourselves or how we want to "see" the world as a result of our actions and their impact.

---

[1] HBR blog: "What's Your Vision of the Good Life?" August 18, 2008

The Import of a Vision Statement

Before we can begin the journey of living as re-singled adults, we must prayerfully create a mental map (our vision statement) regarding where we want to go, who we desire to be, and what we desire to learn during this season of singleness. Embrace this season as a re-beginning or an opportunity for a do-over, a second chance even. However, if we don't have a vision statement to help map our destinations, who knows where we might end up?

I know that side trips can sometimes lend themselves to exciting adventures and new discoveries, but they take us away from our divine purpose. Whether we realize it or not, there is a divine purpose ready to be birthed from our loss. We may choose to write a song, make a quilt, or plant trees in memory of our beloved. Whatever our vision, we need a plan to get to that moment when spiritual transformation can begin. When will that be? Only God knows.

What to Include

But, before writing the actual statement, take a few moments and write down your answers to these questions. Do not cheat. You have to actually write or type the answers so the transformation can commence. In fact, the answers to these questions may find themselves as part of your vision statement.

- What do you find most engaging and fun about living as a single-again adult?
- What really matters to you? What are your values? What are your beliefs about God?
- What is your purpose as a single adult: to share, encourage, persuade, inform, solve problems, entertain, or inspire?
- How do you feel about living alone?
- How do you combat feelings of loneliness?
- What do you desire to achieve during this season?
- What is one thing you want to change about yourself?
- How do you see your ideal day?
- Where are you now along the continuum of loss?
- Where do you want to be?
- How do you get there?
- What do you need to do to make that life that you envision happen?
- How will you alleviate or eliminate the noise, the distractions?
- What is the one thing you can do every day to make these positive changes last?
- In effect, what is your personal vision for life as a single-again adult in a world of pairs?

Mapping the Vision Statement via Focused Free Writing

For starters, engage in a session of focused free writing. This is a prewriting technique to help you generate and organize ideas. You can use the questions in the preceding section to get you started. Here's how to complete a focused free writing session:

- Gather your favorite pen and writing tablet and settle into an ergonomically-comfortable chair, or sit at your computer.
- At the top of your page, write "During this season of my life, I want my vision statement to include_____," then attempt to address the questions from the preceding section.
- Set a timer for ten minutes and write without stopping.
- Do not be concerned about grammar, spelling, correctness, or any of the other "English-teacher" concerns.
- Use vivid and action-oriented verbs.
- Do not worry if you stray from your vision.
- Just write!

Writing the Vision for Your Life as a Newly Re-singled

Now the fun begins. As you draft your vision statement, consider these tips:

- Use vivid and present-tense verbs to capture your imagination.
- Resist the status quo (do what you desire and can afford to do, whether morally, intellectually, or financially).
- Don't fence yourself in.
- Create the life you want for this season.
- Focus on the future but act now!
- Be clear and descriptively clever.
- Paint broad strokes to capture all aspects of your life.

Do I Really Need A Personal Vision Statement?

Still not convinced? Perhaps, these quotable quotes will put fire in your belly to write that vision statement:

Vision without action is a daydream. Action without vision is a nightmare. ~Japanese Proverb

Vision is not enough; it must be combined with venture. It is not enough to stare up the steps; we must step up the stairs. ~Vaclav Havel

A vision is not just a picture of what could be; it is an appeal to our better selves, a call to become something more. ~Rosabeth Moss Kanter

Your vision will become clear only when you look into your own heart. Who looks outside, dreams; who looks inside awakes. ~Carl Jung

Take Away Points

- To create a vision statement, stay focused on what you are doing as a re-singled adult during this season, stay faithful to who you are, and stand firm in your beliefs about yourself.
- A personal vision statement creates paths to your success as a single-again adult as you map your itinerary toward success.
- A vision statement written down and read daily provides a construct for your life and allows the brain to focus on opportunities for success.
- Your positive mental reality will create positive change, and changes in a positive direction lead to the abundant life.

Must-Dos

Begin now! Dream. Then craft your vision statement for yourself as a re-singled adult. Write it below:

Re-singles Rules(s)!

$\mathscr{Re}$-singles Rule #1

Grieve: It's What You Do After

Loss hovers over us like a vulture; the potential for loss is always present. Indeed, our emotional landscapes may be littered with several losses. These may include loss of jobs, careers, possessions, beloved homes, vintage jewelry, memories due to the ravages of Alzheimer's, and/or best friends who moved away. Other losses may include illnesses, financial setbacks, "empty nest syndrome," and life-stage transitions, such as graduations, weddings, births, and deaths. Lastly, losses may include some of the most distressful severed relationships of all kinds, particularly marital disruptions.

Whatever the shape, form, or fashion in which the loss occurs, and whenever the loss occurs, we grieve. That's a God thing. That's how God created us. Grief is normal in the aftermaths of loss. Loss changes people. However, when we take the time to grieve, we are allowing the vacuum left by the loss to be filled with memories. We remember the good and the bad, the happiest of times and the worst. For when we grieve, something divine is taking place within our very souls. In our discomfort, God is providing us comfort as only He can give. Yet, when we grieve, we must grieve well and thoroughly. As Dr. John Townsend states in *Beyond Boundaries,* "A half grief is never a healing grief." So grieve we must!

Grief Reactions

Research from bereavement studies yields some interesting data. First, grief is not an illness, yet normal grief can look a lot like an illness (Balk 2004). In a 2008 article, "Recovery Following Bereavement," P. C. Rosenblatt found that bereavement may "force withdrawal from life, may require treatment and rest, can sap the ability to accomplish much, can reduce awareness of what is going on, may be treated by medical experts, may challenge the immune system, and is in some sense contagious." Simply put, grieving can cause fatigue!

A.W. Love (2007) categorizes grief reactions. The first type of reaction deals with our *emotions.* Are you sad, angry, guilt-ridden, fearful, ashamed, relieved, or feeling hopeless or powerlessness? If yes, then you are emotionally grieving. Next, grief is categorized in terms of our *thoughts.* What are you thinking? Are you having a difficult time concentrating? Are you preoccupied with thoughts of former relationships or your late spouse? Do you mentally replay the circumstances surrounding the death? Or are you trying to ascribe meaning to the death?

Headaches, stomach aches or chest pains, fatigue, nausea, tension, loss of appetite, and the inability to sleep are among the physical *manifestations of grief.* Moreover, crying, being socially withdrawn, battling substance and food addictions, searching for the deceased, and making frequent trips to the cemetery are *psychological reactions* to grief. Finally, *bereavement reactions* may assume the guise of forcing us to question our spiritual beliefs and values. We may begin to reassess our world view and perceived place in the world ("Progress in Understanding Grief, Complicated Grief, and Caring for the Bereaved").

Stages of Grief

Kubler-Ross (1969) lists five-distinct stages of loss: denial and isolation, anger, bargaining, depression, and acceptance. Please note that each of us experiencing grief may pass through the stages in varying sequences and remain in each stage in varying degrees and lengths of time. Mary Lou Cappel and Suan Leifer (1997) write that the process of grief is "more like a jaded staircase, full of ups and downs, leaps forward and slides downward" ("Loss and the Grieving Process"). Other bereavement researchers note that feelings of grief will eventually dissipate and may permanently disappear. Most agree that normal grief reactions should subside after one-two years, in some cases three. Yet, grief researchers warn that if we are still grieving after three years, we may be experiencing complicated grief, where our grief is delayed, incomplete, or unresolved. If your grief lingers longer, talk with a mental health provider, a spiritual mentor, or join a bereavement support group or a small group within your church to work out your grief in the safe confines of others.

Grieving is Work

Trying to avoid grieving by not thinking about the beloved is psychologically inadvisable. We may need to grieve the old images and the unfulfilled dreams before we can create new memories. We may be forced at some point to try to put our lives back together but not before attempting to ascribe meaning to the loss. The loss has meant something to you. Take the time to think about that. What exactly has this loss meant? How has it impacted your life? How can it change your life?

Loss can effect powerful changes if we don't continually dwell on what's missing in terms of the loss or the person. I'm not being insensitive. I know that you will forever miss your beloved spouse. Nevertheless, at some point, we need to come to grips with what our lives can be like in spite of the loss. This is easier said than done, however. Our getting better after loss can't occur without effort. We must work at it! In one sense, we may literally have to roll up our sleeves and tackle those unfinished projects, even if all we do is make some inquiring phone calls. Remember this: inertia stifles; action frees.

In a *New York Times* article, Jane Brody speaks about her experiences as a widow and about her "compulsion to get things done." As she tackled chores around the house, Brody writes that "each accomplishment is empowering" (June 2010). In fact, Richard G. Tedeschi and Lawrence G. Calhoun (2008) in "Beyond the Concept of Recovery," write that one category of post-traumatic growth is the need to tackle new tasks. Indeed, one of the most effective ways to jump-start our recovery is to get up, get out, and get busy. Sometimes, being busy provides us with a sense of accomplishment. With each completed task, we can bask in knowing that we are re-becoming the competent person we have always been. During this season, we just need to be reminded.

Must-Dos

1. Which tasks need your immediate attention? List them below.

2. What one task can you complete that will give you the greatest sense of accomplishment?

3. Plan a start date and a completion date.

_____

4. What one (im)possible task will you complete?

_____

_____

5. How do you feel after its completion?

_____

_____

_____

_____

_____

_____

_____

_____

_____

_____

_____

_____

_____

$\mathcal{Re}$-singles Rule #2

Become Resilient

When I speak of being resilient, I speak of our God-given supernatural ability to return to a different level of functioning after living through an adverse event. When exposed to traumatic or emotionally and physically taxing situations, we manage to improve, or "survive and thrive," in spite of that loss. Dr. Jean Clinton (2008) defines resilience as the condition of being transformed and altered by an experience of adversity. In fact, the resilient person does not return to former states of being but is adapting, recovering, and coping in positive ways ("Resilience and Recovery").

As a child, I got bullied, teased, and taunted a lot. I remember hearing a saying, perhaps my mother taught it to me, that I would repeat daily. Here's how it went: "Sticks and stones may break my bones, but words will never hurt me. I'm rubber, and you are glue; whatever you say bounces off me and returns to you." I didn't realize it at the time, nor have I thought about that until now, but I was developing my resiliency.

I was toughening my resolve to not let others' words define me. I was rubber, so the negative words and insults hurled against me bounced off of me, leaving no extremely damaging effects. More important is the fact contained in the imbedded metaphor: I could bounce back, even from the negative experience of being bullied, and mind you this was decades before bullying in schools got the attention it demands and commands today! Take heed, re-singled adults. You will bounce back after this loss, but only once you complete the soul work.

Resilience Uncovered

At this point, I must share with you some good and bad news about resiliency. The bad news is that resilience can't be taught; it must be learned. The good news is that it can develop and increase as we successfully survive each setback. Researchers note how some people, even children, possess the innate know-how to handle losses and setbacks and then ready themselves for a comeback. Resilient individuals have learned how to cope. Barbara Kingsolver (1995) admits how she was forced to learn this valuable lesson about coping. She writes:

> "Every one of us is called upon, probably many times, to start a new life. A frightening diagnosis, a marriage, a move, loss of a job or a limb or a loved one, ...In my own worst seasons I've come back from the colorless world of

despair by forcing myself to look hard, for a long time, at a single glorious thing: a flame of red geranium outside my bedroom window. And then another: my daughter in a yellow dress. And another: the perfect outline of a full, dark sphere behind the crescent moon. Until I learned to be in love with my life again. Like a stroke victim retraining new parts of the brain to grasp lost skills, I have taught myself joy, over and over again."[2]

So teach yourself joy. Joy comes from the Lord who is our strength. Read the entire book of Philippians, the book of joy and learn new strategies. But know this. Developing a servant's heart is one way to foster joy. Spread joy and find yourself being more joyful. Let the joy flow! More on this later.

Resilience Begins the Recovery

The ability to survive traumatic experiences and bounce back requires faith, and faith is action-oriented. God's word reminds us this: "For as the body without the spirit is dead, so faith without works is dead also."[3] Our futures have been interrupted or lost due to death, divorce, broken engagements, or dreams deferred. Being resilient requires that we develop a positive self-concept and the can-do spirit. And that can-do spirit demands

---

[2] *Hide Tide in Tucson*. New York: Harper Collins, 15-16
[3] James 2:26, KJV

that we take action; in other words, we must take the initiative and get started!

We can believe that we will grow from a traumatic experience, but what are we doing to turn that belief into a reality? It's true. Resilience is important, for it begins the recovery process. If we are grieving, then we will at some point have to redefine and reintegrate ourselves back into life. This means we have to actively participate in our healing and our growth. While we are recovering after bereavement, we should focus on creating a new future, and this requires developing a can-do spirit and moving forward even in spite of our pain.

The ability to bounce back after a setback is to experience post-traumatic growth, which is another one of the demands placed on the resilient individual. Indeed, positive growth outcomes include improved problem-solving skills, maturity, and, in some cases, a clarity about what really matters. After loss, we may question the utility of some old friendships, discard some relationships, and develop new ones. In fact, the process of living after loss is the focus of my first book, *Re-singled Is Not a Four-Letter Word,* which contains positively-oriented strategies to assist us as we focus on saying yes to life after loss.

The emphasis of this book, however, is that of allowing ourselves to be transformed, which usually occurs somewhere along the continuum of grief. To allow ourselves to be transformed by our losses, we have to admit that we must become proactive, redefine our lives, and embrace our futures. We acknowledge that we will never forget the one lost, and we may be comforted by the fact that the loss will irrevocably change our lives, as it should, but only if we are willing and action-oriented participants.

Must-Dos

1. Think about all the losses in your life. Write them below. Rate each loss on a scale of 1-5 in terms of how it aided in enhancing your resilience. A score of 1 means not resilient, and a score of 5 means highly resilient.

2. For each loss, discuss how it affected you. Rate each loss on a scale of 1-5 in terms of how it aided in enhancing your resilience. A score of 1 means not resilient, and a score of 5 means highly resilient. How have the losses affected you positively?

3. Have you experienced post-traumatic growth?

_____

_____

4. What new skills have your learned or new behaviors have you adopted?

_____

_____

_____

_____

_____

_____

_____

_____

_____

_____

_____

_____

_____

_____

_____

_____

_____

5. What advice would you share with other newly re-singled adults?

$\mathcal{Re}$-singles Rule #3

Repurpose and Reposition

When we become single again after years or decades spent in a relationship, we may find ourselves at odds. Once the grieving ends, and we, the bereaved, face an altered relational landscape, we need a new definition of who we are during this season of our lives. When times get tough economically, people concentrate on finding ways to save money; oftentimes, they repurpose and reposition. You have experienced one of the most traumatic life events; you lost a spouse, partner, or long-time companion. You are experiencing some tough times, so do something to create energy and momentum. What works for furniture and accessories may work for you, the single-again adult.

The concept of repurposing refers to reusing or re-crafting furniture and ordinary items into funky and fashionable decorating statements. Stacy Lambe, a community contributor for BuzzFeed, shares twenty-six ideas. Some of my favorites include repurposing a wooden ladder into a bookshelf, a church pew into a headboard, a suitcase into a chair, a bike into a bathroom counter, and leather belts into a chair. To reposition, on the other hand, means to find another position for or, in the case of newly re-singled adults, to change strategies so fullness and completeness can occur.

Repurpose and Reposition Furniture and Accessories

Several years ago, and many months after settling into a new home, I hired two professionals who virtually transformed my primary living spaces from dreary and drab to deliciously inviting. An item used in one room found a new purpose and position in another. The custom-made feather-filled chairs I had purchased for the living room now reside in the family room, their new home. After the repurposing ladies had employed their expertise, I was thrilled with my home, and I didn't purchase a single item—they merely repurposed and repositioned what I owned.

Here's another example. For years, a re-singled friend of mine has displayed a floor-length gold-framed mirror in her bedroom. However, after becoming a practitioner of feng shui, she removed the mirror and placed it on a wall in her bathroom. What had once been a focal point in her bedroom became a practical accessory in another. Again, finding a new purpose for and a new position gave my friend the ambience she wanted in both rooms.

Clean It Up, Get It Out, or Just Give It Away!

The most drastic act of repurposing and repositioning demands that we give things away. Recently, a married friend of mine shared the contents of an article she had read. The article asserted that accumulating items is a form of gluttony. Don't be a glutton! Share your bounty. Clean it up, get it out, or give it away! Have a garage sale or donate items to charity. What had once been taking up space could become a rainy-day fund, a tax deduction, or at its very best, a room you can use any way you choose.

Perhaps the time has arrived. You realize that you need to do some spiritual house cleaning and depart with the effects of your beloved. If you just can't muster the strength or resolve to do so, elicit the help of a loving friend or relative to assist you. There are some things you may never part with— only you know what they are—so don't. Cherish those keepsakes for as long as you need too. In fact, I have kept my wedding band though divorced for decades now. The band holds no sentimental value for me, except as a marker that I was once married and will be again, soon!

Personal Transformations

Traumatic times require a personal transformation. Don't overwhelm yourself by undertaking a total life re-do. Begin slowly. Tackle one aspect of your life at a time. For a season, a close relative lived with me. The cooking, cleaning, concern, and caring, all occurring while I worked fulltime and wrote part-time, soon took their toll on me.

One day, I looked in the mirror, and I was shocked! That person staring back at me was me, but she had aged as if overnight. I didn't like the way I looked. My skin was drab, my chin less firm. I took myself on as a project. First, I purchased some expensive skin cream, promising to lift and firm. Next, since I enjoy group exercise classes, I began there. I started to eat healthier and began to lose weight ever so slowly. One of my biggest consternations is my hair. I'm in a quandary about what to do about my thinning hair. My hair is a project unto itself; it will have to wait!

This need to repurpose and reposition began at the prompting of my daughter who urged me to update my image. Indeed, I was in need of a personal transformation. I needed to repurpose myself from a casually-dressed down college professor to a successful author and life coach. I needed to reposition myself as a serious contender in the already crowded field of life coaching. I needed to utilize my strengths to find my niche, and so can you! But only when the time is right for you.

Must-Dos

1. What life roles are you playing? What are these roles demanding that you do differently?

2. Now write your life script and use the "Pixar Pitch" as found in *To Sell is Human* by Daniel Pink, with a slight modification made here.

My life before loss

Once upon a time

Every day

Until one day

Because if that

Because of that,

Finally,

My life after loss, once upon a time,

Every day,

Until one day,

Because of that,

Because of that,

Finally,

3. Now compare the two versions. Which version do you prefer? Write your answer below.

4. Why are these versions better? Do you see possibilities and potential? Do you feel more hopeful?

Find a trusted friend or a member of your small group
and share your stories. How did you feel after sharing a
version of your life before loss?

What were some if the comments or feedback received?

Share your story about your life after loss. What reactions did you receive?

What emotional healing occurred after sharing your stories?

What you encourage others experiencing loss to write
and share their stories?

_____

_____

_____

_____

_____

_____

_____

_____

Why?

_____

_____

_____

_____

_____

_____

_____

Why not?

_____

_____

_____

_____

_____

_____

_____

_____

_____

$\mathcal{Re}$-singles Rule #5

Make Peace with Yourself

More than 2000 years ago, the angels declared at the birth of Jesus Christ, the Messiah, our Lord and Savior: "Glory to God in the highest, and on earth, peace, good will toward men.[4] Yet, media headlines and Internet blogs proclaim that world peace is not humanly possible. In spite of all this murmuring, don't you dare become discouraged in your heart or in your mind concerning the status of world peace or peace in the Middle East. While we can pray for world peace, we can't control the world. We can, however, take pleasure in the fact that we *can* achieve peace, but only within ourselves.

How Do We Obtain Inner Peace?

Inner peace begins with God and ends with us! Inner peace emanates from being firmly rooted in a set of core values. For me, my core values are

---

[4] Luke 2:14

based on my religious beliefs. First, I know that my Heavenly Father allows events to occur in my life. He is not the originator of these events; He allows me to experience pain for my personal growth. Next, I know that all things work together in my life for my good. I must confess that this truth is a little bit more difficult for me to understand. Sometimes, days, months, or decades may pass before we come to believe this. Finally, I do not fear, nor do I fret—at least I try not to fret too loudly. I just allow. And I learn what I need to know to grow spiritually.

The Connection between Inner Peace and Contentment

Inner peace may be achieved by embracing a posture of contentment. Contentment may be defined as a state of being in between two emotional extremes. A contented person is emotionally balanced. Not being held sway by the joys or disappointments of life, a contented person does not gauge the quality of his/her day by the day's events. This individual delights neither in what could be better nor what is best, but in what's good for his/her soul at the moment. In fact, the contented man or woman lives completely in the present, basking in the here and now.

Living a Peaceful Life

The person living a peaceful life gives no thoughts about past actions or indiscretions of youth. He/she knows that God can use our pasts. Persons with contented hearts will not attempt to foretell the future. Instead they accept God's presents, the gifts inherent in every day. Furthermore, living a peaceful life involves incorporating the spiritual fruit of peace into our lives. Be ever mindful of this fact—to live a peaceful and contented life, we will have to actively pursue "the things which make for peace."[5] And along with this pursuit, do everything that we can to live in peace.

Must-Dos

To live a life filled with peace and contentment, complete this inventory:
1. About what have you been fretting?

---

[5] Romans 14:19

2. What must you do to increase the contentment factor in your life?

3. What gives you a sense of peace?

4. What can you do to live more peaceably with yourself? With Others?

5. What areas of your life bring contentment?

6. Read Philippians 4:11-12.

Re-singles Rule #6

Don't Let Loneliness Linger

When we are in a relationship for any amount of time, we morph into a completely different person. We are no longer single. Whether married or engaged, we are now part of a couple; we are a pair. Our step quickens; we may even smile at strangers, and our whole being radiates an internal joy and peace. But when the unthinkable happens, when a spouse dies, marriage vows are compromised, the relationship disintegrates, or marital dreams are shattered, our walk slows, our shoulders stoop, and our brilliant smiles disappear. Our entire being is shrouded in the blackness and bleakness of grief. We even look grief-stricken as evidenced by our ashen skin and hollow faces.

As I wrote in my first book, *Re-singled Is Not a Four-Letter Word,* loneliness may be among the unintended consequences of loss. Think of that fact this way. When married or involved in a relationship, we had a constant, dependable, and much-loved spouse or companion. Seldom, if ever, did we have to eat a meal alone, travel by ourselves, or attend to the countless maintenance tasks for the upkeep of our personal property, our homes and our cars, our bikes and our boats. Now, that has changed. And we may be experiencing a state that we have not felt before, or in a long time, we are lonely!

Loneliness by the Numbers

Thomas Wolfe admits, "The whole conviction of my life now rests upon the belief that loneliness, far from being a rare and curious phenomenon, peculiar to myself and to a few other solitary men, is the central and inevitable fact of human existence." However, many would rather tell us their ages or disclose a challenging health condition rather than admit they are experiencing loneliness. Societally speaking, experiencing loneliness is considered a social taboo. An article "Loneliness Updated: An Introduction" that I found in a 2012 issue of the *Journal of Psychology* reports that up to 32 % of adults experience loneliness and that up to 7% report feeling intense loneliness. Karyn Hall, Ph. D., writing in *Psychology Today,* posits that a mere 22 percent of people never feel lonely. Does this statistic imply that 88 percent of people do?

Loneliness Does Not Discriminate!

Even in fairy tales, princes get lonely, so they search high and low for a princess, oftentimes, having to rescue her from ferocious dragons. Your colorist or your barber may get lonely as may your banker. In "The Lethality of Loneliness," Judith Shulevitz states that the lonely are not just the elderly, the poor, the bullied, or the different but, she proclaims, "They're the outsiders." Even if just for a season of being an outsider, we may experience loneliness. Furthermore, an AARP 2010 survey found that one out of every three adults aged 45 and older self-reported that they have experienced chronic loneliness.

Amy Rokach, the guest editor of the issue of *The Journal of Psychology* cited above, reports this finding: the loneliest people are those older than sixty-five but younger than twenty-five years old. Allow me to add this fact: the lonely are those who are disadvantaged, disenfranchised, and those temporarily disconnected from their usual social networks due to losses, particularly the relational losses of death, divorce, or promises broken. They may even be the sub-social among us.

Loneliness Can Kill

"Loneliness hastens death." The circumstantial imposition of loneliness can be as deadly as smoking. Alzheimer's, obesity, diabetes, high blood pressure, heart disease, and cancer may be negatively impacted by loneliness. In fact, loneliness is a public health crisis.[6] Dr. Sanjay Gupta, writing a column in *O Magazine,* reported findings from a study conducted by Naomi Eisenberger, Ph.D., who found that loneliness

[6] Judith Shulevitz, p. 26

triggers the same region of the brain that registers pain. Thus, "Tylenol can reduce the pain of heartbreak."[7] The other loneliness related maladies are not as easily lessened; they may need the solace of the soul brought by the presence of others who care about us.

How to Cure Loneliness

Dr. John T. Cacioppo, an award-winning psychologist at the University of Chicago, refers to the "helper's high." He explains the phenomenon like this: "What's required is to step outside the pain of our own situation long enough to feed others. Real change begins with doing." Here are some of Dr. Cacioppo's suggestions:

- Make meaningful connections;
- Develop a circle of supportive friends;
- Commit random acts of kindness: leaving behind change in a coffee machine or helping an elderly person carry groceries;
- Volunteer in a soup kitchen;
- Read to the blind or to children.[8]

---

[7] Shulevitz 29
[8] Jane E. Brody, "Shaking off Loneliness" NY Times, May 13, 2013

Even the Lone Ranger Had Tonto

Research indicates that widowers, in particular, may isolate themselves from the company of others. They choose to be alone. However, being alone to grieve is not the same as its psychologically more healthy cousin, temporary withdrawing to be still in solitude and to heal. Solitude is that state that allows us to gain perspective, to reminiscence about the good times and regret the bad ones. But loneliness, on the other hand, is not a desired state. Loneliness saps our strength, depletes our spiritual reserves, and makes us more susceptible to illness. The point is this: though both 'lonely' and 'solitude' mean being by oneself or a state of aloneness, to experience solitude is a blissful state in which we can reflect, reminiscence, revitalize, and reaffirm our faith in God and His Goodness.

A third option may work. Elicit the support of a trustworthy friend and talk about your loss. Talking it out will lessen the pain of loss; the more you talk, the more you heal. Encourage those who are grieving; offer them 'time to whine' and a strong, steady shoulder on which to cry. Performing a relationship post-mortem, especially in the case of a negative divorce or breakup, will heal the relationship wounds faster. So find your Tonto today.

Must-Dos

1. What are some specific strategies you can employ to stave off loneliness?

2. Complete this progress chart:
Random act of helpfulness

Date Completed

3. Describe some instances in which you experienced a "helper's high." What were you doing? Who were you helping?

_____

_____

_____

_____

_____

_____

_____

_____

4. Now ask yourself this: When you were truly engaged in a cause larger than yourself, how many times did you feel lonely?

_____

_____

_____

_____

_____

_____

_____

_____

$\mathcal{R}e$-singles Rule #7

Toss Your Head and Attract Ted or Suck in Your Gut and Strut

Scientifically speaking, humans and animals, including both males and females of the species, instinctively know how to flirt. The word "flirt," according to its etymology, comes from *fleureter,* a French word meaning to "touch lightly." Joan Ellison Rodgers, writing in *Psychology Today* asserts that flirting is nature's way of helping us attract and choose the right mate. In fact, attracting a potential mate is vital to the survival of the human species. Flirting is serious and sociologically significant. Undertaken as a topic worthy of study about three decades ago, flirting has yielded a plethora of information, from flirting behaviors to understanding how and why we flirt.

Flirting Behaviors

Actions ranging from smiling, looking at a stranger and then turning away, or tilting one's chin downward and to the side are all flirtatious. The best analogy I have of flirting is having a picture taken by a professional photographer. This happened to me when I took a photo for an employee directory. I sat on a stool in the photographer's studio, knees to one side. The photographer asked me to tilt my chin downward and then turn my head slightly. He asked me to smile. I was not flirting. However, I was engaging in a form self-promotion at the photographer's bidding. He wanted to capture my essence from my best angle. This is the purpose of flirting—to put our best selves forward. And why not? For we are fearfully and wonderfully made in His image, and we praise Him (Psalms 139:14, paraphrase).

So, when we flirt, we are showcasing ourselves physically. But what about showcasing ourselves spiritually? Speaking at a women's conference, a minister noted that men are attracted to women who have a pretty face—whether natural beauties or those with skills to use makeup to enhance their natural beauty. But, he continued, some men are drawn to women who are spiritually attractive. In fact, spiritual attractiveness emanates from a man or woman when he/she is passionately possessed with an enticingly-enriching endeavor. It matters not if we are starting a business or teaching a Sunday school class for pre-school aged children. What matters most is the active pursuit of pleasurable pastimes. But don't worry if you are too busy to undertake another single task. Here are some flirting strategies that might work for you.

Be Serenely Confident

Choose to rule! Declare today that you will serve God by possessing joyfulness and gladness for the abundance of all things (Deuteronomy 28:47, paraphrase). In fact, some of the most intensely interesting men I have met seem to live by this. One widower in particular was what I will call the strong, silent type. His "joyfulness and gladness" showed in the fact that he rarely complained—no matter what the circumstances or the burdens being carried upon his shoulders. He was thankful that the circumstances were not as bad as they could be or as bad as those burdens being shouldered by others. He was grateful that he was not the one needing help. He was thankful to God that he was in a position to give help, if needed. This attitude made him serenely confident and more attuned to others. It really upped his attractiveness factor as well.

Ask the Right Questions

When I was growing up, both men and women often asked one another they met for the first time: "What's your sign?" Now considered comical, this question is outdated. At the time, knowing one's zodiac sign was supposed to have portended compatibility. Asking the right questions can be great conversation starters, however. These are the type of "security" questions being asked when we need to create a password. So if we are going to rule as re-singles, develop a list of questions to ask someone upon meeting him/her. Questions, such as "What is your first childhood memory?" or "Who was your favorite teacher?" are sure to break the ice and set the stage for enjoying a great conversation with a person we deem interesting and worthy of getting to know better.

Be an Active Listener

The Bible tells us to listen twice as much as we speak. James 1:19 states, "Wherefore, my beloved brethren, let every man be swift to hear, slow to speak, and slow to wrath." This is excellent advice. But listening is not the same as hearing. Hearing is automatic unless one is hearing-impaired. Listening, on the other hand, requires conscious concentration, so our brains can make sense of the sounds we hear. To be a better listener, look at the speaker. Really listen with intent, not to correct, evaluate, or interrupt. Just listen! Giving someone else our undivided attention can be flirtatious in itself. Everyone, no matter how successful or not, deserves, make that, desires to be heard!

Must-Dos

1. Flirt! Honestly answer this question: "How many times in the last month have you flirted?" If you answered, "None"; then learn how to flirt. Read book or articles on flirting. Ask the most successful flirters you know to coach you in the art of flirting.

2. Develop an action plan. We learn when we do. What specific steps will you take? List them below:

$\mathscr{Re}$-singles Rule #8

Become a Dating Dynamo

Are you all dressed up with nowhere to go? Are you weary and worn from living as a re-singled in a world of pairs? Are you frightened by the thought of being forever re-singled? One "Yes"! might signal your readiness to date. Dating! The dreaded d-word! For a re-singled, one of the most daunting and fearful, yet potentially fun, activities is a date. Before you put on that new outfit, before you accept that first date, let's complete some dating prerequisites.

Are You Ready to Date?

If you are still dealing with an abundance of emotional distresses, then you may want to delay dating a while longer. You may have to wait until you can deal with the feelings of rejection and inadequacy that may result when a first date doesn't lead to a second one. Perhaps, you need to delay dating until you are emotionally stronger and well-grounded in a sense of self.

Why Do You Want to Date?

Be intentional. Before heading out the door, take a moment and decide now why you want to date. Do you desire companionship? Do you want a traveling partner? Are you ready for commitment? Remarriage? As you become more immersed in dating, your purposes may change; nonetheless, being mindful of your purpose is crucial! Whatsoever you desire, your thoughts, your attitudes, and your behaviors will make happen.

Get the Word Out

An anonymous proverb states that "he who has a thing to sell and goes and whispers in a well is not as apt to get the dollars as he who climbs a tree and hollers." Before you protest too much, allow me to explain. Think of yourself as a commodity—a rare jewel of a person. Yet, if you keep your generosity and all you can bring to a relationship to yourself, you are in fact whispering in a well. To get more dates, tell more people! In fact, climb that tree and holler! Tell your friends, family members, co-workers, your doctor, your lawyer, and even your pastor. Inform any and all who will listen about your intentions to date. Be daring! Ask them to set you up on a blind date, and then assure them that you will not burden them with any dating details or blame them for dating disasters.

Go Back to School

Learn as much as you can about dating. Read books, articles, and blogs about dating. Take notes and follow the wisdom contained therein. Learn how to read body language and facial expressions. In fact, researchers note that 55 percent of what we communicate occurs via body language. Learn to listen. Listen for what's being revealed as well as for what's being concealed. Then, too, taking a community-education class at a local college could net you several potential dates. The men or women enrolled in these classes share at least one interest of yours—the subject matter. What's being discussed in the class could at least become an ice-breaker and fodder for conversation over cheesecake and coffee after class. I know several couples who met in college classes, and I suppose you do too. There's something to be said about learning and loving, especially learning to love.

Keep an Open Mind

Hang out with a different crowd of people. A wise widow told me that she doesn't go out with women's-only groups. She insists that to hang out with women sends men the wrong message. Think about it this way: what man is really all that confident to approach a group of women? When this widow, I'll call her Ava, goes out, she prefers mixed company, couples even. She is not intimated in the least about being a "third wheel." Dating is not for the timid or mild-mannered. Be bold and brazen! Actively seek out those you want to date; no stalking is allowed, ever!

Tally-Ho

Keep a tally of your dating successes and failures. If one date doesn't lead to more dates, don't despair. Change! Here's what I suggest. Keep a notebook, tallying the types of dates in terms of the enjoyment factor. Include basic facts, such as who-what-when-where-how. When you return from the date, or the next day, ask yourself two simple questions: What did you like best about the date? What would you do differently? Over a period, a pattern will emerge; you'll make adjustments and become a dating dynamo in no time.

What Do We Do If…?

Finding the right person is a matter of timing, and dating ups your opportunities for getting there, wherever there is for you. One of the biggest turn-ons is that person whose entire essence is infused with hope, peace, joy, and genuine love. Take these fruits of the Spirit (Galatians 5:22-23) with you everywhere you go, whether you are dating or not. In a world filled with darkness and dread, you can be that beam of light shining in your sphere of influence. These "sweet meats" of the Spirit are certain to attract the right person into your life at the right time.

Must-Dos

Make a list of all things positive that you take on a date. Write them below:

$\mathcal{Re}$-singles Rule #9

Share Your Story

Like you, I have suffered numerous losses. During losses, our belief in God can be a source of solace or a source of suffering. For many, God comforts us in our sorrow. Religious rituals, prayer, and surrounding ourselves with spiritually-minded friends can help ease our sorrow. For others, their loss may cause a rift in their relationship with God. These have prayed, asking God to heal their loved one, yet he/she died in spite of the fervent praying. Others may stop attending church services or reading their Bibles. These may "swear off" religion—at least temporarily.

In fact, during times of our most intense suffering, if we can engage in religious and spiritual activities, we may accrue psychological benefits. We may feel closer to God, become less depressed, and see anxiety dissipate. Instead of experiencing a religious rift, we may actually grow spiritually, experiencing a closer connection with God and a deepening relationship with His son Jesus, as well as "spiritual connectedness with others."[9] This increased awareness of our place in the world, and God's presence in our lives during our sorrowing, reminds us that all things work together for good to them that love God, to them who are the called according to His purpose.[10]

Finding Meaning: A Manifesto

Loss smashes dreams and derails plans. Indeed, loss can interrupt life and set us on a collision course with chronic depression. For some, loss can become a religious struggle as they attempt to integrate the loss into their lives. One of the best strategies that works for me is to engage in countless hours of introspection, to be still. Other researchers, however, advance the notion that to try to understand life's events, we need to construct "frameworks of meaning." These frameworks help us figure it all out in terms of our place in the world and our purpose. Furthermore they state that the underpinnings also shape our goals and expectations. But the researchers remind us that loss upends our frameworks.

After loss, we are compelled to find ways to integrate the loss into our meaning systems. Celeste M. Johnson summarizes the constructivist conceptualization of bereavement. This approach is primarily concerned with meaning making. To conceptualize is akin to thinking about the loss and the effect of the loss upon the individual. Johnson

[9] Pargament and Raiya, 2007
[10] Romans 8:28

asserts that when we conceptualize, we engage in a process. When we experience a loss, we grieve and then find a way to reconstruct the loss and ascribe meaning to the loss. Finally, we are able to use the loss to aid in personal transformation. In this regard, those grieving are actually writing a story of loss.

The Power of Personal Narratives

Jerome Bruner, in "Life as Narrative," acknowledges that told stories are recipes for structuring experience. "Lived time," he asserts, is best expressed though narratives. To construct a narrative is, in itself, a sort of "life making" (1987). These stories, specifically those dealing with loss, are not passive, but "affectively and idiosyncratically affect each listener, at the time the tale is told and later." Narratives suggest "myriad pathways out of dark forests."[11] Stories foster perspective-taking via numerous modalities: stories have relational ways of connecting, explanatory ways of knowing, creative ways of creating reality, historical ways of remembering, and predictive ways of visioning the future. [12] In essence, stories provide a safe space for encountering the strongest of emotional experiences and for providing templates for healing.[13]

---

[11] Sunwolf & Frey, 2002
[12] Sunwolf & Frey, 2002
[13] Diving in the Moon Journal, Issue 3, Spring 2002

Sunwolf, Ph.D. (2002), speaks about the health benefits emanating from telling stories as well as listening to them. When we hear negative narratives, we feel luckier by comparison. Positive stories, in contrast, serve as role models and offer hope ("Grief Tales"). Kimberly King knows about the grief and rage that are the twin faces of sorrow. She suggests that our culture lacks grieving rituals. Without these outlets for sorrow, our emotions are like "lions in the kitchen; we pretend they don't exist—they don't go away if ignored; they get hungry, angry, and dangerous." So how do we keep the lions at bay? We share our stories of loss and hope and healing.

Must-Dos

1. Write your story of loss.

2. Why did you write the story that way?

3. Rewrite as a story of hope.

4. What story told helped you heal?

Re-singles Rule #10

Cry Out to God!

The New Year ushered in weeks infused with joyous times and a commitment to revolutionize my life. I detoxed my body by fasting from caffeinated coffee and chocolate. I was basking in a supernatural state of I-can-do-this, until...Well; suffice it to say that from the highs of those first few weeks, I began a descent. Perhaps, the ambitious attempt to fast from a potent addiction to caffeine was the culprit. I'm not exactly sure what happened, but something sure did! I quickly bottomed-out. I descended deep down into a darkness that lasted one desolate winter weekend.

I tried my usual remedies to assuage my emotional turmoil. I baked chocolate brownies and indulged myself. But not before I had walked five miles on the treadmill. Mindlessly, I watched hours of television. I napped. I watched more television. I drank chamomile tea as I sat in the bed reading my Bible.

The next day was Sunday. Intending to attend church services, I awoke too late and too psychologically drained to rush to church. Was the culprit all the sugar I had consumed or my emotional state? It didn't matter. The anomie remained. Needing to seek comfort in The Word, I decided to watch the services of the church I frequent as it streamed live on the computer. But of all Sundays, the services wouldn't stream. I tried several times. I relented, accepting this as a divinely-inspired symbolic wink. Something more was needed.

Truthfully, at this particular point in my life, I harbored a lot of angst and pain after the deaths of my mother and my stepdad, occurring two years and one day apart. But the final blow was to my mother's legacy when I learned that my stepdad had bequeathed the family home and the possessions he and mom had accumulated to the caregiver. I lost it. I started to weep, and the tears flowed and kept on flowing. For a span of time "I watered my couch with tears" (Psalms 6:6b). Before long, I slipped into a state of self-pitying despair. Desperately, I cried out to God and laid bare my soul on the altar, not a real altar but the metaphorical one on the floor beside the daybed in my office. And it didn't take long. God heard my cries, and He answered me! The resulting catharsis cleansed and healed me from all of those repressed emotions.

The Lesson Learned

Why do I share this with you? It's because at some point along your journey to healing after loss you will experience something supernaturally divine, something so transforming. The bereavement researchers and others may not tell you this, but it happened to me, and it may happen to you. You are going to get to a point, after you have tried every other solution, that you will be forced to cry out to God.

Cry Out to God!

I'm calling this the confess-profess-then-protest phase of healing. When we confess, we stop lying to ourselves. We are willing, to borrow a term from pop culture, to lay our cards on the table and say, "You win." We are willing to admit to God "whose ways are higher than our ways and whose thoughts are higher than our thoughts" (Isaiah 55:9) that we need His supernatural strength and the indwelling discernment of the Holy Spirit. To profess is to take our confession a step further. For when we profess, we are agreeing with our confession. In effect, we do two things. First, we acknowledge the hurt. Second, we admit to ourselves and to God that we desire that the pain stop. To solidify the process, we cry out to God, for we know that if we are going to get better, we must verbalize our confessions and profess our action plans!

In our anguish of lying prostrate on the altar of the Almighty, we experience remorse and shame, perhaps guilt, and are finally ready and willing to acknowledge that it's time. Finally, to protest solidifies our decision of surrender. For with our protesting, we, as Dr. John Townsend writes, are giving voice to our negative feelings and pain. We simply get to a point where we are forced to relent and decide then and there that "I've had enough. I will face my life head-on, and I will succeed with God's grace." Once this phase ends, we can then recover, redefine, and reintegrate ourselves back into life.

Must-Dos

1. Share one instance when you had to cry out to God.

2. What prompted the outcry?

3. How long after the loss did the outpouring occur?

_____

_____

_____

_____

_____

4. What were you experiencing at the time? What else was going on in your life?

_____

_____

_____

_____

5. Describe how you felt afterwards.

_____

_____

_____

_____

_____

_____

_____

6. What did you discover?

_____

_____

_____

_____

_____

_____

_____

_____

7. What, if anything, did you resolve to do?

_____

_____

_____

_____

_____

_____

_____

_____

_____

$\mathcal{Re}$-singles Rule #11

Refuel Your Joy

In my first book, *Re-singled Is Not a Four-Letter Word,* I advised readers to choose to be happy. According to positive psychology, we can do this by focusing on positive things that happen to us, even the serendipitous ones like finding a parking space, especially on those days when we are running late. We can find opportunities to help others, and we can thank God for the blessings He has bestowed upon us. Yet, to experience a deep, divine connection to the eternal, we must refuel our joy. To achieve that "peace that passeth all understanding," (Philippians 4:7), we need to go beyond the happiness boundary and cross over into joy. Joy will be forever present when we walk "through the valley of the shadow of death" (Psalm 23:4) and work out the death of a beloved spouse or a relationship.

So what? Who cares?

Happiness is fleeting. It could be here one minute and gone the next. We could be feeling happy (blessed, fortunate) then, with one stray negative thought, we could be questioning our good fortune the next. For happiness is circumstantial. What this means is that our happiness is generated from what happens to us or what is done to us. Happiness is passive. Without a doubt, our happiness is at the mercy of what happens in our lives. If we choose to be happy, we must choose to not give sway to those circumstances over which we have no control. Circumstances are what they are. Circumstances do not define us: they are not who we are in Christ. Nor do they determine our outcomes.

While we may be thinking that happiness and joy are synonymous, joy, on the other hand, is so much more. For you see, joy is Christ-centered, according to Chris Hodges, pastor of the Church of The Highlands, Birmingham, Alabama. When we give our lives to Christ, we receive a supernatural transformation. Our focus shifts from the external world to the internal condition of our souls, which is our goal as Christians, a goal with an eternal, heavenly reward.

Secondly, in our joy, we are not immune from trouble. Loss cannot evade us. But we have a heavenly advocate who has overcome the world. That is great news! That's the gospel truth that transforms. Remember, we are overcomers. We can and will come over and out from under the yoke of our present loss. Another thing that Christ may teach us is to share our joy. As we are blessed and become healed, we should share our stories with others who are now walking the path of loss that we once walked.

Finally, in our joy, God will speak to us; He may even reveal a purpose or a mission. This is what happened to me. For decades, I pleaded and bargained with God, imploring Him to send me a Godly husband. Instead, God has sent me a mission, a ministry to help other re-singles regain their surefootedness and find love again, if that is their desire. As God speaks to us through the Holy Spirit, He will reveal paths where we can find hope in spite of dark places. As I write this, I still have no husband, but I do bask in my God-given joy, so that I can serve as a role model and remind others to rejoice in the midst of our circumstances. "Rejoice in the Lord always: and again, I say, Rejoice" (Philippians 4:4).

Must-Dos

1. Don't ever stop praying, believing, hoping, and encouraging others.

2. Confess your faults to another, and pray for one another that they may be healed (James 5:16).

3. Know that God is the solution.

4. In your struggles, seek opportunities to bless others.

_____

_____

_____

_____

_____

_____

_____

5. Add your own joy-filled activities below:

_____

_____

_____

_____

_____

_____

_____

_____

_____

Re-singles Rule #12

Lighten Up!

Don't despair. This rule is not about losing weight, eating healthy, or exercising. But it could be. Perhaps, it should be. Nevertheless, during this season of your life, you must take care of yourself. But, for some of us, during this season, our 'god is our stomach.' Alas, I digress. When I yell, "Lighten up!" I'm talking about humor, more specifically about the need to develop a sense of humor. Admittedly, I struggled with writing this rule. It has caused me much consternation and aggravation. I wrote, erased, rewrote, had several false starts, and then stopped. When I mentioned this to my daughter, she wisely retorted, "Mom, you're having a difficult time because there is nothing humorous about being re-singled."

That's a fact! Being a single-again adult in a world of pairs is like being the odd-person on the team. It reminds us that "two's company, but three's a crowd." And who wants to stick around some place where they're not wanted? Certainly not me! Everywhere we look, people are paired up, but we are not. The stark reality puts a grid lock around our hearts and places a stronghold in our minds. And yet? Nothing, except this. God's word tells us, "These things I have spoken unto you, that in me ye might have peace. In the world ye shall have tribulation: but be of good cheer; I have overcome the world" (John 16:33). The mere act of typing this verse comforts me and causes me to smile. Does this mean that I have a sense of humor?

What is This Thing Called a Sense of Humor?

Two distinct meanings attach themselves to the phrase "a sense of humor." My reaction to typing John 16:33 is a classic example of the first meaning of a sense of humor. In this case, a sense of humor is not illusive, but denotes the Omnipresence of God. It suggests how watching a wind hover glide through the air can bring joy to our souls. I let the joy flow as I notice that a Kildee has returned for the second year in a row to build its nest in the tiniest patch of grass in *my* yard. In fact, we can adopt the posture of a six-year old and sense the presence of things that make us laugh like chasing a kite through the air.

More readily known, however, is the sense of humor or a giftedness that some individuals possess. These folks make us laugh. For years, I have worked with a colleague who has an innate sense of humor. Whenever he shares an everyday occurrence, before I know it, I am bowed over, laughing. But I also have a sense of humor, as I appreciate a good joke or an amusing anecdote when I hear one. Another colleague shared that a friend of hers gave up wine for Lent but choose to drink hard liquor instead. I laughed heartily when I heard the irony contained in that.

Why Humor?

God has a sense of humor. We are made in His likeness; so logically, we all have a sense of humor, or at the very least, should develop one. So, you're not convinced that God has a sense of humor? Or perhaps, you never thought about God in this way? In fact, the Hebrew Bible abounds with instances of God's humor. According to Hershey H. Friedman, Ph.D., (2000), *God laughs!* and several examples can be found in the Psalms: Psalms 2:4, 37:13, 59:9.

Dr. Friedman posits that the Hebrew Bible uses a variety of humor, not to entertain but to teach lessons and to demonstrate the profound negative consequences that befall wrongdoers. According to him, the humor in the Hebrew Bible takes these forms: sarcasm; irony; wordplays, double entendres and puns; humorous names and imagery; exaggerations, stories, and situations. Dr. Friedman posits that the Hebrew Bible is replete with instances of humor for the sole purpose of bringing us closer to God. This reminds me that when man plans, God laughs. So let go; let God, and laugh!

When We Laugh, We Heal

Perhaps the best example of the healing power of laughter is the case of Norman Cousins, the author of *Anatomy of an Illness* (1979) and the inspiration behind humor therapy. The former editor of *Saturday Review,* Cousins was diagnosed with a degenerative illness after returning from Russia. The diagnosis? Cousins had six months to live. After careful deliberation, he surmised that if stress had exacerbated the disease, then feeling less stressful could cure him, perhaps. For two weeks, Cousins watched all things humorous. His prognosis? Doctors eliminated his medication, and Cousins was well enough to return to work in six months. And most surprising is that Norman Cousins lived for sixteen more years.

For three decades, Dr. William Fry has studied humor and its effects. He compares laughing to "inner jogging" and notes that laughing 100 times a day equals ten minutes spent on a rowing machine. Moreover, laughing increases the heart rate, improves blood circulation, and works muscles.[14] Tait Russell reports that cardiologists at the University of Maryland Center in Baltimore found that laughing, along with a sense of humor, may stave off a heart attack. One of the lead researchers, Dr. Michael Miller, says that laughing helps to make our blood vessels healthy and protects the heart. For these reasons, "He who laughs…lasts."

---

[14] "The Respiratory Components of Mirthful Laughter." Journal of Biological Psychology, 19, 39-50

Even work environments are being infused with humor. Many offer professional development sessions on using humor at work. This has sparked a growth in "humor consultants" who suggest ways to make working more fun and less stressful.[15] What works on our jobs may work in our homes. How can we create an atmosphere in our homes where we laugh with each other and not at one another? The bottom line is this: indulge in self-care, lighten up, and laugh, for "a merry heart doeth good like a medicine, but a broken spirit drieth the bones" (Proverbs 17:22).

Must-Dos

1. Write down all the funny memories you have of the deceased.

---

[15] Puder, 2003

2. Share these funny stories with others.

3. Become a humor magnet. Look for ways to infuse your life with laughter.

4. Become intentional and influential about engaging others in laughter.

5. Hijack conversations. Begin each conversation with something funny or positive.

6. Keep humorous props on hand to share with those who visit your office if you still work or for the grandkids whenever they visit.

7. What are some specific strategies you can undertake to spread humor? Write them below:

Re-singles Rule #13

Break All Rules, Except the Ones You Keep!

All of our lives, we've been given rules to follow. As children, our parents told us not to touch the stove because it was hot, to look both ways before crossing the street, to eat our vegetables, to never talk to strangers, and to share with others. Even teachers got in the act. They admonished us if we colored outside the lines, were just too busy reading Nancy Drew or The Hardy Boys to complete our homework, or failed to complete 50 pushups in ten minutes.

As an adult, we have lived by another set of rules. "Go to college, so you can get a good job." Once we got a job, we were supposed to arrive early and stay late, work harder to get ahead, work longer to stay ahead, buy a house before buying a car, save more than we spend, and on and on. Civic laws keep us safe, and the rules of etiquette instruct us about how to behave. Netiquette tells us how we are supposed to behave when we use a computer at a college, a university, or even a public library.

Rules and the Re-singled Adult

When we became re-singled adults—whether through death, divorce, or a broken engagement—we had to learn how to complete tasks that we once took for granted. When was the last time you had to take the car to have it serviced? While married, when did you ever have to arrange to have the lawn cut? Or what about the dripping kitchen faucet? Can you fix that drip? Not only that, you may be trying to live out your re-singled status according to someone else's rules.

For the longest time, I've heard so many married women friends say to me, "If something ever happens to my husband, I'll never marry again." I bought into that, and for the longest feigned no interest in wanting to remarry. By the time I realized that I had been duped by someone else's rule, I had let many years pass and had ignored several potential suitors. Take it from me. It's okay to break the rules.

Some Rules Are Meant to Be Broken!

Rules work! We must obey the laws or suffer the consequences. Rules and laws keep us safe and try to protect us from ourselves. But do we really need all of these rules? Rules may also constrain and constrict us. Must we always stay within the lines when we color, or is it okay to extend the boundaries, to enlarge our perspectives? Is it socially acceptable, or at least, personally gratifying, to push the edges? For isn't that where creativity resides? Trying to live out our loss and create a positive and fulfilling life for ourselves may require some rule-breaking. Here are some rules that may need to be broken:

- Older women should not wear their hair long.
- You are too old to wear bright red lipstick; a muted shade would work better.
- Men should never wear pastel shirts and ties.
- Hang out with people your own age.
- Why don't you retire and move to be closer to your grandkids?
- Isn't it time you downsized to a smaller house, car, etc?
- Know your place.

One Rule You Should Keep!

Go out to the tip of the limb! To go out on a limb means to take a risk, to be bodacious and doggedly determined, daring even. Being out there on the tip of the limb is scary, yet it can be refreshingly challenging. We can see a lot from there, but what we will see are things from a different perspective—one of balance. Balance. As a re-singled adult, balance is what you will need, at least during the first couple of seasons. You work hard at putting your life back together; then you rest. You give; you get. You experience life as newly re-singled; you learn remarkable life lessons. For it is in dying to self that we truly live in Him!

Must-Dos

1. By which rules have you always lived?

2. Was there ever a time in your life when you broke just one rule? What did you do? What was the outcome? Were you pleased with the outcome?

3. As a re-singled adult, you need to attend to the *tasks* of grief. These include accepting the reality of loss, experiencing the pain of the loss, adjusting to a new environment, and re-investing in a new reality.[16]

As you confront each task, what rules might you need to break?

---

[16] PsychologyTools.Org., based on Worden's tasks of mourning. Worden, J. W. (1991) Grief Counseling and Grief Therapy, 2nd edition. London: Springer

4. As you write your own rulebook, which rules will you include?

_____

_____

_____

_____

_____

_____

_____

_____

_____

_____

_____

_____

_____

_____

_____

_____

Please share your new rules with me; my Email address is wynoradwf@yahoo.com.

eferences

Achor, S. (2013). *Before Happiness* Audiobook. New York: Crown Business.

Balk, D. E. (2004). Recovery following bereavement: metaphor, phenomenology, and culture. In P. C. Rosenblatt, (2008). *Death Studies, 32*, 6-16.

Bowman, T. (1999). Shattered dreams, resiliency, and hope: "restorying" after loss. *Journal of Personal and Interpersonal Loss, 4,* 179-193.

Bruner, J. (1987). Life as narrative. *Social Research 54,* 11-32.

Cappel, M. L. and Leifer, S. (1997). Loss and the grieving process. *Parks & Recreation, 32.5,* 82. MasterFile Premier. Web. 7 Feb. 2013.

Clinton, J. (2008). Resilience and recovery. *International Journal of Children's Spirituality, 13,* 213-222.

Friedman, H.H. (2000). Humor in the Hebrew Bible. Humor: *International Journal of Humor Research, 13.3,* 258-285.

Hall, K. (2013). Accepting Loneliness. Published on Psychology Today. (http://www.psychologytoday.com)

Johnson, C. M. (2010). The constructivist conceptualization of bereavement. *Omega, 61,* 121-143.

Kelley, M. and Chan, K. T. (2012). Assessing the role of attachment to God, meaning, and religious coping as mediators in the grief experience. *Death Studies, 36,* 199-227.

King, K. (2014). The twin aces of sorrow: stories that help heal grief. The Healing Story Alliance website.

Kubler-Ross, E. (1969). *On Death and Dying.* New York: Macmillan & Co., Ltd.

Love, AW (2007). Progress in understanding grief, complicated grief, and caring for the bereaved. *Contemporary Nurse, 27,* 73-83.

Paletti, R. (2008). Recovery in context: bereavement, culture, and the transformation of the therapeutic self. *Death Studies, 32,* 17-26.

Pargament, K.I. and H. A. Raiya (2007). A decade of research on the psychology of religion and coping. *Psyke & Logos, 28,* 142-166.

Puder, C. (2003). The healthful effects of laughter. *The International Child and Youth Network, 55*. Online at http://www.cyc-net.org.

Rokach, A. (2012). Loneliness updated: an introduction. *The Journal of Psychology, 146*, 1-6.

Rosenblatt, P. C. (2008). Recovery following bereavement: metaphor, phenomenology, and culture. *Death Studies, 32,* 6-16.

*Scripture references are from the King James Version of the Bible

Shulevitz, J. (2013). The lethality of loneliness. The New Republic at http://www.thenewrepublic.com/article/1131 76/science.

Sunwolf & Frey. (2002). Grief tales: the therapeutic power of folktales to heal bereavement and loss. *Diving in the Moon Journal, 3.* Online.

Russell, T. (2008). Healing Humor. *Saturday Evening Post, 280.4.*

Tedeschi, R. G. and Calhoun, L. G. (2008). Beyond the concept of recovery: growth and the experience of loss. *Death Studies, 32,* 27-39.